BORN AND BREWE

*Quips and pump clips from independent
Yorkshire breweries accompanied by
humorous verse*

Born and Brewed

IN YORKSHIRE

by Rosie Walker

From Whitby down to Sheffield
Over hills and vales,
Across from Hull to Huddersfield
Over moors and dales.
A county blessed with beauty,
For all good things are here,
Not only perfect scenery
But also lovely beer!

Wharncliffe Publishing

First Published in 2001 by
Wharncliffe Publishing
an imprint of
Pen and Sword Books Limited,
47 Church Street, Barnsley,
South Yorkshire. S70 2AS

Copyright © Rosie Walker 2001

*For up-to-date information on other titles produced under the
Wharncliffe imprint, please telephone or write to:*

**Wharncliffe Publishing
FREEPOST
47 Church Street
Barnsley
South Yorkshire S70 2BR
Telephone (24 hours): 01226 - 734555**

ISBN: 1-903425-14-X

A CIP catalogue record of this book is available from the
British Library

Printed by ColourBooks Ltd., Dublin

CONTENTS

I had my first pint of real ale in 1991 and after $3^1/_2$ pints was legless! The next morning, experiencing the most dreadful hangover, I felt like death warmed up! Since then I have become an avid follower of real ale, so much so, I decided to compile a book on my favourite pastime, pump clip spotting. I was a newcomer to the varieties of beer available, not really knowing which beer to taste next, always depending on the opinions of others more experienced in the art of quaffing. The only guideline I had to expanding my newly awakened taste buds was the picture on the clip that adorned the pump on the bar. I have the same problem betting on horses, if the name sounds right and the horse looks nice, I back it. So if the pump clip awakened my curiosity in what the taste would be, I took a gamble that the beer would live up to it's name. Moving on from simple names like Best Bitter and Dark Mild, to beers with names I could not even mention in this book, I have become somewhat of a connoisseur on pump clips, always on the lookout for a good piece of artwork and imagining the story behind the name. That's when the little rhymes started buzzing in my head, (or was it the effect of the alcohol!) It was so fascinating that I decided to look into each one in more detail. Why call it that name? Was there a weird and wonderful story behind it? Who brewed it? Where was the brewery? And so the quest began. I am amazed at the results I have found.

There are over 45 independent breweries in Yorkshire alone and hundreds of others busy producing excellent real ales all over the country. My scribbles on the back of beer mats have led me to a greater knowledge of brewing and the history of Yorkshire. This small sample has been put together hoping to open your eyes to the inner soul of the humble pump clip. From one small piece of plastic, card, or even enamel, the pump clip tells a story that is as good as the taste of the beer. So Cheers! Smile a bit, learn a bit, drink a lot and more than anything, ENJOY!

A BRIEF HISTORY OF THE PUMP CLIP

As far back as when time began, labels were used to describe any product. When few people were literate, a picture or a symbol would show the consumer what to expect. Imagine living in the time of the Saxons. The smell of a rough brew of hops and malt steaming away in the pot over a roaring campfire. Beside it stewed root vegetables bubbling furiously. Thirsty warriors longing for a drink would not want to make the mistake of supping a pint of broth instead of a strong concoction of alcohol. So the pots would be simply labelled STEW with a picture of vegetables, and BREW, a picture of a smiling face. Hence, they knew which was which. As the centuries passed more people preferred to drink than eat and taverns appeared all over the country. The pub was born! As ale developed, more detailed descriptions were needed and the picture pump clip was invented to express the character of the taste. Anyway, that's my story!

On a more serious note, it is thought that the pump clip was first introduced in the 1950's, although there are some simple examples before the second World War. With the introduction of modern illuminated signs for mass produced beers and lagers, the pump clip was rarely seen. As more micro breweries emerged, the need to distinguish one ale from another became increasingly important. Each brewer, wanting to make their beer more attractive than another, would design elaborate pump clips to tempt the customer. Sometimes engraved on wood or brass, the pictures would portray local heroes, folklore characters, or scenes from the area. Today, the range of pump clips is tremendous and have become collectable items. They not only inform us of the brewer and the strength, but also illustrate an overall view of the beer. Each pump clip holds a story, truth or fantasy. Start spotting and use your imagination.

In the words of the strongest Yorkshire ale, brewed at the Frog and Parrot Brewhouse in Sheffield, 'Roger and Out'.

A shepherd came a' calling by,
The lambs were all brought in,
The evening frost was crisp and white
And sparkled on his skin.
The village pub was all lit up
The log fires burning bright,
He downed a pint of Riggwelter
And soon he felt alright.
Warmth spread through his frozen bones
He drank six pints of beer,
And then he fell onto his back,
His legs up in the air!

Riggwelter

Strong Yorkshire Ale

A.B.V. 5.9%

Situated at the gateway to Wensleydale where sheep roam free across the hills, the brewery has it's own small flock of Hebridian Welsh cross sheep, six ewes and one ram. The word Riggwelter is derived from the old Norse language brought into Yorkshire by the Vikings. Rygg - meaning back, and Velt to overturn. When a sheep is on it's back and cannot get up without help, the local Dales people say it is rigged, or riggwelted. Since Riggwelter is a 5.9% beer, too much could possibly cause the same effect for a human if several pints of this strong ale are consumed!

BLACK SHEEP

WENSLEYDALE

Riggwelter

Strong Yorkshire Ale

A.B.V. 5.9%

The Black Sheep Brewery is owned by Paul Theakston, the fifth generation of Masham's famous brewing family. The actual brew house was installed in 1992 and sits in what was the kiln of the old Lightfoot Brewery which Paul's grandfather took over in 1919. It is laid out in the traditional tower fashion, whereby mashtun, copper and hop back are positioned one above the other, with gravity taking the brew down through the process. The brewery runs shepherded tours where the visitor can not only see, smell and taste the beers produced, but also dine in the welcoming atmosphere of the Black Sheep Bistro.

The Devil's Knell

On Christmas Eve the lads were out,
Heads spinning round with ale,
But passing by the churchyard
Their skin turned ghostly pale,
For there they saw Sir Thomas,
His eyes were black as coal
He cried "Please help me strangers,
And save my sorry soul!
I miss my pint of English ale
I cannot stand this hell!
Hurry up and set me free,
And ring that bloody bell!"

Sir Thomas de Soothill was Lord of the Manor. He had a wicked temper and during a fit, murdered a servant boy. He hid the body in Forge Dam nearby. When he had calmed down and realised what he had done, he was afraid of going to hell. To save his soul, he gave Dewsbury Minster a 13 cwt. tenor bell with the instructions that it should be tolled every Christmas Eve, once for every year since Christ's birth. The bell is called Black Tom and bears the inscription: 'I shall be here if treated just, when you are mouldering in the dust'. Tolling the Devil's Knell at Dewsbury still takes place every Christmas Eve.

The Devil's Knell
4.8% ABV
BLACK TOM
The Anglo Dutch Brewery
DEWSBURY, West Yorkshire

The Anglo Dutch Brewery was set up in November 2000. It gets it's name from a Dutchman and Englishman going into partnership. Paul Klos was born in Holland. In the 1960's, when home brewing was illegal there, Paul would take a trip to England four times a year to buy malt. He wanted to learn the craft of brewing and when offered a job with Rother Valley Brewery in Sussex, left Holland in 1995. He finally met up with Mike Field, owner of the West Riding Refreshment Rooms at Dewsbury railway station, and they formed the new brewery in a former dye house in the town.

Dracula arrived one night
Upon the Whitby shore
Followed by his big black dog,
They passed the old church door.
Dracula was thirsty
And to the graveyard sped,
His big black dog wandered off
And found a pub instead.
He howled until they let him in,
The landlord he did shout…
"Here's a dish of bitter lad
Drink up, and then get out!"

whitby's black dog

first out

ABV 4.0%

The name 'First Out' relates to the story of the arrival of a black dog in Whitby. Many years ago a ship was wrecked on the beach. All of the crew were dead, the only living creature was a large black dog that was seen leaping from the wreck and running up the 199 steps to St Mary's church. He must have passed the brewery and called in for a quick pint while Dracula headed for the graveyard!

The logo and name for The Black Dog Brewery were inspired by Bram Stoker who, having spent time in Whitby on holiday, went on to write the most famous horror novel of all time, Dracula, first published in 1897. The Black Dog Brewery was opened in 1997 and is situated in an old workhouse on the east cliff, close to the 199 steps leading to the famous abbey. Many of it's beers are distributed all over the North of England.

Deep below the city walls
Underneath the ground,
T'was heard a dreadful moaning,
A ghostly, wailing sound.
There, stirred the soul of Cedric
A soldier from old times,
Who lost his life in battle
From drinking beer and wines.
He lay beneath the brewery
Where the sweet smell of hops
Awoke him from his slumber -
Up from the ground he popped.
"Give me a pint of good ale!"
He cried into the night,
And still he is a wandering,
A melancholy sight.

The old city of York holds many legends, the greatest being that of the 'lost legion'. In Roman times many men were killed in battle and whole armies were lost, their fate sealed to wander the walls of the city for all time. Recently, while in the brewery cellar, a plumber had a rather scary experience. He saw a Roman Legion marching across the floor but their lower legs appeared to be below ground level. It has since been discovered that the brewery building is built above a Roman road, hence the feet of the Roman legion were treading firmly on Roman soil several inches below! If you fancy ghost spotting take the York Brewery tour.

YORK BREWERY

the York Dungeon

Special Millennium Brew

in association with York Dungeon

Centurion's Ghost Ale

5.0% ABV

The ghostly lost Roman Legion of York
Dead for 2000 Yrs, doomed to patrol the city for all eternity

YORK'S ONE AND ONLY

Y ork Brewery was established in 1996 and has since expanded to include an opportunity to see a traditional brewery in full operation. It houses a 20 gallon brew plant with four 20 barrel fermenters and ten conditioning tanks. A full range of quality beers are brewed here and distributed all over the country. A delivery of bottled beers has been sent as far afield as Canada. It has an olde-worlde style bar that is rich in history, displaying maps and pictures of life in the old city of York and there is a gift shop where memorabilia of the brewery can be bought. Centurion's Ghost has recently been upgraded from 5% to 5.4%

The wind was howling in the hills,
The night was dark and cold,
And in the local village inn
Some gruesome tales were told
About the great white horse that's carved
Up on the hillside high,
And that sometimes at midnight
You'll hear his piercing cry.
His hooves beat hard upon the ground,
He thunders down the dale,
You're sure to meet this awesome sight
If you drink too much ale.

Hambleton Brewery is close to the site of the White Horse, carved into the hillside at Kilburn by a local schoolmaster and his pupils in 1857. The picture of the horse was made by cutting away the turf to reveal the white limestone underneath. This ancient art of turf cutting, called leucippotomy, goes back many centuries, the first recorded is thought to have been made by the Danes in 878. There are many giant horses and crosses in England, and similar land drawings can be seen all over the world. A trust fund was left to ensure that the Kilburn Horse does not become overgrown and the artwork lost forever.

H ambleton Ales, situated on the banks of the river in the tiny hamlet of Holme-on-Swale, a few miles west of Thirsk, was founded by Nick Stafford and his wife Sally in March 1991. Initially the brewery was based in converted outbuildings in Sally's parents home until 1994 when, owing to the expansion of the business, it moved to it's present location. Brewing methods are very traditional using the finest malted barley from East Yorkshire and Northdown hops. The local water is perfect for producing a finely balanced and refreshing beer which has a unique flavour.

Nell the elephant took a stroll
And wandered off one day,
She ended up aboard a boat
That sailed her far away.
The young Empress of India
On hearing the bad news,
Was distraught, and cried aloud
"Well! We are not amused!"
But Nell is quite contented,
Although a little drunk,
She's partial to a glass of beer
In which to dunk her trunk!

This beer was named after the Empress of India pub that opened in 1822 in Northgate, Wakefield. It was demolished in 1938. Queen Victoria was given the title Empress of India in 1876. Although this poem is dedicated to Queen Victoria and the Indian elephant, please forgive the poetic licence when you view the picture opposite. It is actually an African elephant. How can you tell the difference? An Indian elephant has smaller ears. The female Indian elephant does not have tusks. Also, if you ever get close enough to notice, the Indian elephant has only one finger-like protrusion on the tip of it's trunk, whereas the African elephant has two.

Fernandes Brewery was designed and built by David James. It produces excellent beers ranging from a beautiful dark mild called Malt Shovel, also named after an old Wakefield pub and one of my favourite beers, to Empress of India 6% abv and Double Six 6% abv. The pub above the brewery not only offers a good range of Dave's beers and several guest beers but has a genever gin bar offering over 24 flavours. The delicacy of genever is not only for the ladies – the biggest and burliest of men can be seen sipping from one of the delicate special glasses, raving about the taste of 'Fruits of the Forest' alongside their well pulled pint!

Down at Wakefield Rugby club
The fans were roaring loud,
Mike Harrison had stole the ball
And raced across the ground.
"Come on Mike! Now score a try!"
He thundered to the line,
But the thought of Clarks good beer
Was all that filled his mind.
He dropped the ball, ran to the gate,
The crowds they shook their heads,
As he disappeared from view
To steal a pint instead!

Burglar Bill, a full bodied ale with a rich and malty taste, was brewed to celebrate local rugby hero Mike Harrison being made England's Rugby Union captain in 1987. The team played the All Blacks in New Zealand at the first Rugby Union World Cup. Mike became well known for his speed and skill on the rugby pitch, always 'stealing' the ball from the opposition. The All Blacks gave him the nickname of Burglar Bill which stuck with him for the rest of his career.

MIKE HARRISON'S SPECIAL BREW

BURGLAR BILL'S

Brewed by

CLARKS

of Wakefield

ABV 4.4%

Clarks Brewery was established in 1905 by brewer Henry Boon Clark who, a year later, was joined by a local businessman to form the company HB Clark & Co (Successors) Ltd. Over the years, despite the introduction of pasteurised beers in the 1960's, Clarks expanded and a new custom built brewery was commissioned in 1982. In the same year Clarks Traditional Bitter was voted the Best Bitter of the Year at the Great British Beer Festival. Clarks also has an extensive cash and carry shop stocking a wide range of beers, wines and spirits.

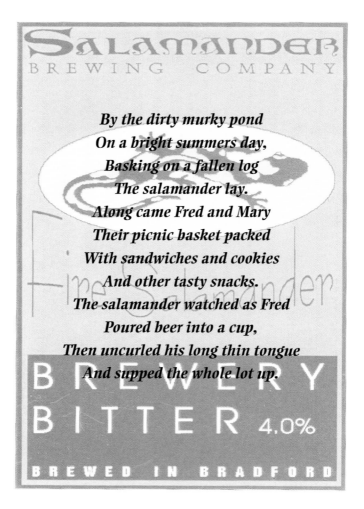

SALAMANDER
BREWING COMPANY

By the dirty murky pond
On a bright summers day,
Basking on a fallen log
The salamander lay.
Along came Fred and Mary
Their picnic basket packed
With sandwiches and cookies
And other tasty snacks.
The salamander watched as Fred
Poured beer into a cup,
Then uncurled his long thin tongue
And supped the whole lot up.

BREWERY
BITTER 4.0%

BREWED IN BRADFORD

Salamander (Salamandridae) are a group of about 400 species of amphibians that have tails. Ranging from the smallest newt at four inches to the Chinese salamander at 5 feet, they are found near fresh water ponds in deep woodlands. Although most salamanders are mainly terrestrial, they like moist conditions and return to water to breed. Eggs are laid in masses and remain in the larval stage between a few days to a few years depending on the type. Gills close and a sticky tongue pad forms. In some cases, for example the Mud Puppy, metamorphosis does not complete and they retain their larval features.

SALAMANDER
BREWING COMPANY

Fire Salamander

BREWERY
BITTER 4.0%

BREWED IN BRADFORD

C hris Bee and Daniel Gent spent between January 2000 and January 2001 preparing their brewery in the derelict premises of the Dehners Pie factory. Bradfordians will remember this famous delicacy of thirty years ago. No longer will the smell of a good pie waft from the building, but an aroma of hops and malt as the production of real ale takes place. The fermenting tanks were formerly dairy tanks and being stainless steel are ideal for brewing. The name of the brewery was inspired by a tapestry of the coat of arms of Francois I featuring a colourful salamander.

With anoraks and waterproofs
And good tough sturdy boots,
The lads trekked up the hillsides
Through heathers and dead roots.
But then the heavens opened
With thunder and with rain,
Said Mick, "I'm really soakin',
I'll not come here again!"
But through the misty valley
A pub came into sight,
And soon they felt much better
With a sandwich and a pint.

The Three Peaks consists of Whernside, Ingleborough and Pen-y-ghent all of which are around 700 metres high. They cover 160 square kilometres of limestone uplands in the Yorkshire Pennines and are part of the Pennine Way. The 24-arched Settle to Carlisle railway viaduct spans across the boggy moor at Ribblehead. Over 12,000 people climb Ingleborough each year, reaching the Iron Age hill fort on the flat topped summit. The annual fell running race covering 24 miles is run every April and for those who yearn for a tougher challenge, the Three Peaks Cycle Race takes place every autumn.

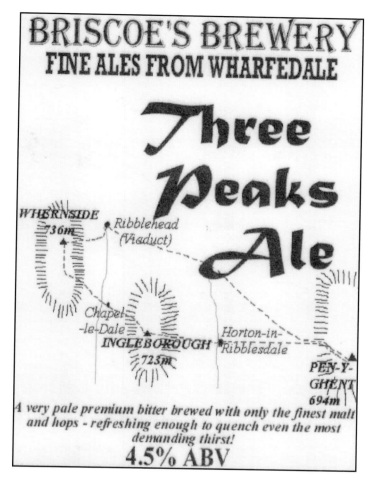

BRISCOE'S BREWERY
FINE ALES FROM WHARFEDALE

Three Peaks Ale

WHERNSIDE 736m

Ribblehead (Viaduct)

Chapel -le-Dale

INGLEBOROUGH 723m

Horton-in-Ribblesdale

PEN-Y-GHENT 694m

A very pale premium bitter brewed with only the finest malt and hops - refreshing enough to quench even the most demanding thirst!

4.5% ABV

Briscoe's Brewery was started in 1998 by Paul Briscoe who is a qualified biochemist. The brewery is much a one man band with the emphasis being on quality rather than quantity. As Paul is a serious long distance runner, most of his beers are named along this theme. The brewery is behind the Bowling Green pub at Otley, an unique experience in itself. Inside, the pub houses not only Briscoe's excellent beer but also an array of unusual items including a full skeleton by the pool table. For those suffering from arachnophobia, beware the pet tarantula behind the bar! But don't let this deter you – it's friendly!

A gale was blowing, seas were high
The sailors all felt sick,
"Captain Scoresby save us please
And find a harbour, quick!"
He scrambled to the crow's nest
The wind ripped through the sails,
And at the top he thought he saw
A glimpse of Yorkshire Dales.
"Land ahoy!" he cried out loud,
"A haven is in sight!
Hold on to your stomachs lads,
We'll drink some ale tonight!"

William Scoresby was born in Cropton on 3rd May 1760. He worked on his fathers farm until the age of nineteen when he went to Whitby as an apprentice on a ship called The Jane. His career as a sailor led him to many adventures, one being aboard the Speedwell where he was captured by the Spanish. Luckily he escaped on an English ship and returned to England. In 1785 he was back at sea aboard the Greenland whaler The Henrietta, under the leadership of Captain Crispin Bean. In 1790 he took over as Captain and gained fame for his skills in catching whales. He is best remembered for his invention of the safe lookout at the top of the mast known as the crow's nest. A monument to this great sailor can be seen in Whitby.

CROPTON BREWERY

SCORESBY

ABV 4.2%

STOUT

CASK CONDITIONED

Records show that ale was brewed in the tiny village of Cropton as far back as 1613. The brewery owes it's existence, in part at least, to a deep seated local fear that one day, during the harsh moor winters, the beer wagon might not be able to find a way through. This being too serious a prospect for most regulars to contemplate, steps were taken to safeguard the village beer supply, whilst at the same time, providing the locals with an exclusive beer of unique character. From such humble beginnings (and slightly suspect motives!) the brewery's products have progressed to win national recognition among real ale drinkers.

The ale was flowing, fast and hard
The locals drank it down.
They'd finished off the barrel when
Dick Turpin came to town.
He roared when Bob said "Beer's all gone
These lot have drunk me dry,
I ll not have time to change it now
I bid you sir, goodbye."
Dick pulled his musket from his coat
And aimed it at poor Bob
And then he shot the barrel through
And swallowed the last drop.

Dick Turpin was the son of an alehouse keeper. Found stealing cattle, he fled to join a gang of deer rustlers and smugglers in Essex. When the gang broke up he went into partnership with Tom King, a highwayman. There are several stories of their conquests along the roads of old England where they brought terror to all who travelled the highways. While firing at a constable he accidentally shot Tom King. Once again he fled the arm of the law and went to Yorkshire where he set up business as a horse dealer under the name of John Palmer. Turpin was finally convicted at York Assizes for horse stealing and hung in 1739. Hence he experienced 'his last drop!'

The most recent addition to York Brewery's ventures is the opening of it's first pub in August 2000. The Last Drop Inn is located in a 17th Century building on Colliergate which has been extensively refitted to give a relaxing environment in which to sample a wide range of the brewery's beers. For those wanting to escape the wild noisy bars of today's modern living and take a step back in time, the Last Drop Inn is a traditional ale house in which to enjoy a pint of real ale and good wholesome food, made with local ingredients.

RUDGATE

The Viking he came charging in
With axe and shield in hand,
Roared, "Landlord fetch me good ale
Brewed in this foreign land!"
With one great gulp, he swilled it down
And grabbed the barmaid's waist,
"By 'eck this is a crackin' beer
It's really got some taste!"
He blew his horn and called his mates
From far across the sea,
To build a Viking settlement
At Rudgate's Brewery.

VIKING

abv 3.8%

By Rudgate Brewery Ltd - York.

The naming of 'Viking' is purely imaginative, as is the above verse. However, based on the Viking influence in this particular area, one can envisage these wild men arriving on the shores of Yorkshire, tired, parched and hungry. The vision of thousands of Nordic warriors tramping the lanes around York gasping for a drink inspired this verse. Use your imagination to feel their delight in finding a watering hole that provided them with a satisfying pint of real ale! Then the battle that must have commenced to win over this fruitful land that could provide them with the drink of the gods!'

Rudgate started brewing in October 1992 operating from one of the buildings on a disused airfield at Tockwith near York. It is believed that an old Viking pathway runs through the area, hence the Viking theme on many of the beers that are produced here. Viking, Battleaxe and Ruby Mild are brewed all year round, with a different beer made each month of the year, plus occasional special brews. Others on the Viking theme include Hagar's Mash, Thors Best, Eriks's Ale and Olaf's Pride. For a 3.8%, Viking is a beer full of body with a fruity aftertaste.

"M'Lud, I didn't do it Sir!"
The murderer did cry,
"But if you have to hang me,
One wish before I die.
Let me go outside the gate,
I know that I am doomed,
I need a jug of Clarks real ale
Out there at Henry Boons."
The judge he donned his black cap,
The death bell it did chime...
"Well mine's a pint before you hang,
You've got till closing time!"

The rear entrance to Clarks Brewery is on Back Lane, opposite Her Majesty's Prison Wakefield, hence the naming of this beer. In 1965 the death sentence was abolished and a life sentence took it's place. Despite two motions in Parliament to restore it, it was never brought back, although it is still an issue that is raised occasionally. Death was formerly the only penalty for all felonies in English law, although pardons were given to offenders if they were willing to be transported. Execution was normally carried out immediately, and the judge wearing his black cap was a sure sign that there would be no mercy.

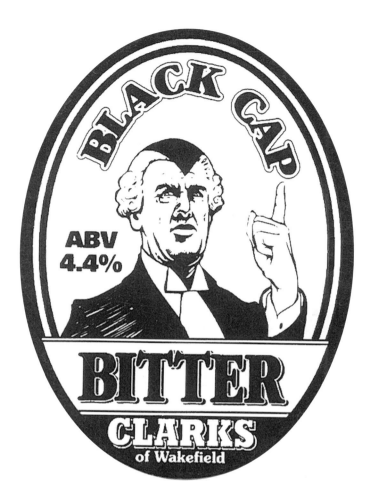

C larks Brewery also houses Henry Boon's alehouse, a popular drinking place in the town. Unfortunately for the inmates of Wakefield Prison there is no connecting tunnel! Henry Boon's has always been a popular stop off for those who 'do the Westgate Run' – a beer drinking experience well known to Wakefield folk. The abundance of pubs along this street has brought many a good night out for the lads. Other good stop off points to sample Clarks beers are Boons of Horbury and The Kings Arms at Heath Common, Wakefield, both traditional pubs.

The Concertina band was sad
Their leader had the flu,
They were playing for the King
And at the Palace due.
They tried him with some asprin
But it just made him sick,
But then young Archie Watson said
"This'll do the trick!"
He poured a pint of strong dark ale,
Bandleader drank it down,
In minutes he was on his feet
And off they went to town.

Concertina Best Bitter is dedicated to it's namesake, the Mexborough Concertina Band that used the original premises. The band was founded in 1886 and went on to be top winners of a national competition held at Alexander Palace in 1906. They were then invited to play at a concert for Edward VII. The band used to play brass band music on their concertinas. Tchaikovsky actually composed a piece especially for this instrument. Sadly, there are very few Concertina bands around nowadays but the memory lives on in this small Yorkshire brewery. Incidentally, Archie Watson is the last surviving member of the band.

BEST BITTER

3.9%ABV

CONCERTINA BREWERY

The Concertina Brewery, run by Andy Pickering and brother-in-law Alan Boyd, is situated in Mexborough South Yorkshire. The original building was a wooden structure which was owned by Mexborough Concertina Band, hence the brewery name and the particular beer pictured. In 1920 the building was extended and bricked in and now houses the bar on the upper floor and the brewery in the cellar. The building was bought in 1987 and brewing started in 1992. They brew six regular beers, including Bengal Tiger which won the Champion Beer of Britain bronze medal in 1997, and occasional special brews.

The cave was dark and gloomy
And John was most upset,
He'd gone down in the pot hole
Just for a drunken bet.
But now things looked much different,
He wished he'd stayed int' bar,
Drinking ale and eating nuts
Was much more fun by far.
He scrambled up the rock side
And climbed towards the light,
His mates gave him a pint of beer
And soon he felt alright.

Lost John's is one of several caves in the Leck Fell area of the Yorkshire Dales. It is 141 metres deep and 6 kms long. There are three major routes down, all meeting at a traverse called Battleaxe. The cave is liable to serious flooding and roaring torrents combined with loose boulders makes this a dangerous cave to explore. It is recommended for groups rather than solo pot holers. Lost John's is connected to several other caves in the area including Notts Pot, Rumbling Hole, Lost Pot and Boxhead Pot.

**Invented and brewed in
Goose Eye at the Turkey Brewery**

LOST JOHN'S

ALE

ABV 3% to 6%

Named after Caves in the Yorkshire Dales

The Turkey Brewery at Goose Eye near Keighley, (not to be confused with the Goose Eye Brewery,) started brewing in September 2000 and now produces several different ales. All of the beers are named after caves in the Yorkshire area due to Harry Brisland, the brewer, being a keen caver. The brewery is behind the 200 year old Turkey Inn pub where part of the hillside at the back has been dug away to accommodate the brewery building. The walls are four feet thick and I imagine that Harry feels well at home in his own brewing 'cave'.

The train had left for Newcastle
It thundered down the track,
A streak of silver lightning
Streamlined on its back.
The driver grinned with pleasure,
"Eh! What a great machine!
To drive this lovely engine
Has always been my dream."
It sped through England's counties
Till Yorkshire came to view,
The driver said "We'll stop right here
They do a right good brew!"

The Silver King LNER 2511 was one of four LNER A4 Pacific locomotives built in 1935 that ran from London Kings Cross to Newcastle. They all had 4 small wheels on the front, six driving wheels in the centre and 2 wheels on the back and were the first streamlined trains. All four engines were originally painted silver to celebrate the Royal Silver Jubilee. The other three trains in the silver theme were Silver Link LNER 2509, Quicksilver LNER 2510, and Silver Fox LNER 2512. Ossett Brewery has beers named after them all.

O ssett Brewery started brewing in 1998 behind the Brewers Pride pub on Healey Lane Ossett. It now brews between 15 to 25 barrels a week and has a constant range of 6-8 beers available. A year after opening, Silver King won the Beer of the Festival at the 1999 Leeds CAMRA Beer Festival and since then the brewery has gained additional awards. The pub used to be a Clarkes pub which was called Boons End due to the fact that Healey Road stops at the pub. Prior to that, it was the Millers Arms.

King Charlie came a wandering
In search of real good beer
To take it back to London Town
And bring his folks some cheer.
Down at the local brewery
The Yorkshiremen were sad,
The thought of running out of ale
Would make them all so mad !
They called the city Governor,
John Hotham was his name,
He said, "Get out of Yorkshire lad,
And don't come back again!"

The Hotham family originated from the village of Hotham near North Cave and was one of the most influential in Yorkshire. Sir John Hotham was knighted by James 1 at York. In 1625 he was elected into the first Parliament of Charles 1 and appointed Governor of Hull in 1628. Hotham gained disfavour from King Charles for his critical attitude in Parliament and dared to offend the King by refusing to allow soldiers to enter Hull. It is said that this event contributed to the start of the Civil War.

THE GOVERNOR

SIR JOHN
HOTHAM

THE HULL
BREWERY
COMPANY

ALCOHOL
VOLUME
4.4%

STRONG ALE

The name of the closed Hull Brewery was resurrected after a 15 year absence when a new brewery opened in 1989. It was forced into liquidation in 1994 and the assets taken over by a local businessman who formed the new company. The brewery is situated in one of the old fish smokehouses near the city. A bottling plant was added in 1997. Passengers on the North Sea Ferries from Hull to Holland can enjoy Hull Brewery Premium and Bitter on board, making their trip even more enjoyable.

DALESIDE BREWERY

For fifty years old Jack had sped
Across the Yorkshire Dales,
He'd jump stone walls and rivers
In search of tasty ales.
Eventually he grew so old
He could not run a mile,
He tried and tried but could not get
His leg over the stile.
And so he hung his old boots up
And passed the time away
Drinking ales from Daleside
Every single day.

OLD LEG OVER

4.1% ABV

"A RIGHT GRAND YORKSHIRE BEER"

There are vast acres of beautiful countryside in the Yorkshire Dales. Fell-runners have to leg over thousands of stiles, stone walls and streams in pursuing this traditional sport. One old runner won three races in one day in the 1920's, another won more than 100 races over thirty years. Over 300 fell-runners take part on Haworth Moor every New Year's eve for a bottle of Yorkshire ale. Old Leg Over is dedicated to all fell-runners. A medium dark, well balanced traditional beer, the main hops are Northern Brewer and Hersbrucker.

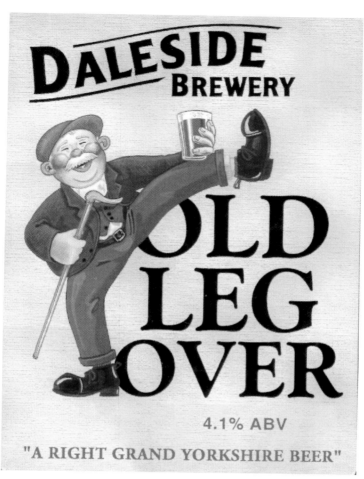

DALESIDE BREWERY

OLD LEG OVER

4.1% ABV

"A RIGHT GRAND YORKSHIRE BEER"

Daleside is associated with the Witty family whose tradition in brewing goes back more than 600 years to the time when their forebears arrived in England in the late 13th Century from Belgium. The Brewery is situated in Harrogate, the Victorian spa town famous for it's healing waters, on the edge of the Yorkshire Dales National Park. Bill Witty established the brewery in the mid 1980's and moved to the present larger premises in 1992. The whole brewery was installed with new equipment and re-organised in June 2000.

The pub was full of shouting
The boys had had a few,
They'd been down to the bookies
And won a quid or two.
The landlord gave a warning
And loudly he did shout,
"Unless you stop your yelling
I ll chuck you beggars out!
You're banned until tomorrow,"
He gave an evil glance,
"I've told you once. I ll tell you twice
You've had a double chance!"

The naming of Double Chance holds a fascinating story. In the early 1920's two horses were stabled at the Crown coaching inn. When the owner was given the bill he was unable to pay and instead offered one of his horses to the landlord. The chosen horse earned it's keep by pulling the taxi carriages from the local station to the town. However, had Mr Suddaby chosen the other horse he would have been a far richer man. Lt J P Wilson, a well known steeplechase jockey rode Double Chance to victory in the 1925 Grand National. Thus the name was adopted by Malton Brewery for their premium beer.

DOUBLE CHANCE · MALTON BREWERY

OG 1036°-40°

Malton Brewery operates from the rear of the Suddaby's Crown Hotel in Malton. This former coaching inn was acquired by William Suddaby in 1878 and has been in the family ever since. In 1984 the late Bob Suddaby, Geoff Woolons, a retired brewer, and Colin Sykes, an industrial chemist, founded the Malton Brewing Company and converted the old stables into the present premises where the fermenting room now stands. The brewery is now run by the Suddaby family with Alan Brayshaw as brewer. The Crown is an ideal location to enjoy the North Yorkshire Moors, a brewery trip and good ale.

"Flippin eck, I'm flamin mad
I'm really quite flummuxed!
I'm fairly sure I fixed that fence
With nails and screws and nuts!
But now my cow has bolted
And I am right fed up,
I think I'll finish work today
And get a pint t'sup!"
So off Fred went to Filey,
But on the way he found
His brown cow in the brewery
Laid drunken on the ground.

abv5%

Brewed at Brown Cow Brewery
Selby, North Yorkshire. Tel: 01757 618947

Old E'fer, was brewed to celebrate the 66th birthday of Colin Bernard who works at the brewery. Colin is well known for his rather 'expressive' language, never completing a sentence without having to use 'that' word. The other heifer refers to cattle, being a young virgin cow. In ancient times heifers used to be used in sacrifices, being valued for their purity. In Greek mythology Zeus fell in love with Io, first priestess to his wife Hera. When his wife found out, he changed Io into a heifer to protect her and she escaped to Egypt where she was restored to her original form.

Old E'fer

abv5%

Brewed at Brown Cow Brewery
Selby, North Yorkshire.   Tel: 01757 618947

The Brown Cow Brewery at Selby is run by Sue Simpson, one of the few female brewers in the country. The brewery was named after Sue's home, built around 200 years ago which was originally the Brown Cow pub. Sue started brewing as a hobby and after working as a secretary for sixteen years, decided to start her own brewery. Taught by a master brewer she learnt the different aspects of commercial brewing and how to run a business. Brewing takes a lot of physical energy, but Sue has succeeded in turning a hobby into a successful venture. The brewery now produces around 7 barrels a week.

Herbert went off for a walk
To get a breath of air,
The sun was hot, his brow was wet
He fancied a cool beer.
So called into his local
And there did quench his thirst,
He drank and drank until he thought
His tummy it would burst!
He stumbled to the tow path
To find his way back home,
But fell into the nettles
And stung his big fat bum!

When John Eastwood brewed a new beer he asked for suggestions for a name. One customer told him that Eastwood was also the place where D. H. Lawrence was born. Apparently Lawrence indulged in 'nettle-thrashing' and actually wrote a poem called 'Nettles' in 1930. It all sounds a bit sadistic to me, but there may be a medical reason behind this weird practice. Nettles contain a high content of histamine which can expand the blood vessels in the body. Beating them on the skin enabled active constituents of the immune system to pass through and fight injury or infection. Don't try this at home!

The brewery is owned by White Rose Inns and is situated alongside the Barge and Barrel pub. John Eastwood, has been brewing for over 7 years and his beers supply local free trade as well as the White Rose Inns. The original building was the Station Hotel, built in the early 1900's. Between the railway and the canal it was a convenient point for travellers from Manchester to stop off on their visits to the Yorkshire woollen mills. The Barge and Barrel is on the banks of the Calder and Hebble Navigation and still offers excellent hospitality to visitors by road, rail or barge.

The metal clanked as cog wheels turned,
The men stood on the street,
They had no jobs to make them brass
And had no bread to eat.
Said Joe, "Lets pop down t'the pub,
We have nowt else to do,
Half a crown will see us right
And buy a beer or two!"
They drank till they were tipsy
A gallon they did sup,
Then grabbed a great big hammer
And smashed the mills all up!

In 1812, after 20 years of war with France, England faced high unemployment. The 'Croppers' in the woollen mills who put a smooth finish on cloth were replaced by machinery and morale was low. Taking matters into their own hands they raided the textile mills and smashed the machines that had put them out of a job. They blamed the damage on a mythical General Ludd and became known as the Luddites. Ironically the hammers they used to destroy the machines were made by Enoch Taylor, who also made the machinery. Hence the local saying, 'Enoch hath made them, Enoch shall break them'.

Linfit Brewery operates at The Sair, a brew pub in the village of Linthwaite, pronounced 'Linfit', near Huddersfield. One of the stories behind the name of the pub, originally called the New Inn, tells at the turn of the century the landlord brewed some beer that turned 'sour' or 'sair' as the local people pronounced it. Since then the pub has held that name. Needless to say the current landlord, Ron Crabtree, does not follow in his predecessors footsteps as his beer is always top quality! Another story of the naming of the Sair, is that it is the Colne Valley pronunciation for the word pig, or sow.

The cuckoo he was singing
To herald in the Spring.
"Hey!" said Tom, "Let's build a wall
To keep that birdie in!"
And so they started building,
But just when they were near
To putting stones upon the top
Tom said, "Let's have a beer!"
They went down to the tavern,
And there they stayed all day
But while they all got plastered
The cuckoo flew away!

Ruffled Feathers was brewed especially for Cuckoo Day which is celebrated every Spring in Marsden. Local legend says that many years ago the people of Marsden noticed that the cuckoo heralded the arrival of Spring and good weather. They thought that if they could capture the cuckoo, then they could also capture Spring and the village would always be bathed in sunshine. A group of local men searched out the cuckoo and finding it in a tree, built a high wall around it. They were just about to put the last stone on top when the cuckoo flew away. As the local legend says "it were no'but just wun course too low!"

RUFFLED FEATHERS

A Specially Brewed Beer

Riverhead Brewery Tap

4.5% ABV

Riverhead Brewery is situated in Marsden town by the side of the river Colne. The brewery used to be the old Co-op grocery store which was converted to a brew pub in 1995. Brewing takes place on the pub premises and seven regular beers are produced. Some of the beers are named after local reservoirs, the strength of the beer resembling the depth of the water, (the stronger the beer the deeper the reservoir it is named after). It also brews occasional beers such as Jazz Bitter, which is brewed especially for the annual Marsden Jazz Festival, and Ruffled Feathers for Cuckoo Day.

All across the Yorkshire Dales
The heather was in bloom,
Attracting all the honey bees
With it's sweet perfume.
They settled on the flower heads
And sucked the nectar dry,
Then off to find their beehives
Swiftly they did fly.
But passing by the brewery
The smell of fresh sweet hops
Tempted them to change their flight
And there the bees all stopped.

S ean Franklin asked his two young children, Sam 6 and Joe 5, to design this special pump clip for 'Nectar' producing an excellent result! Heather covers miles of the Yorkshire Moors and Dales, it's purple hue in full glory during late summer. It provides a feast for the honeybees as they collect nectar for their hives converting it into honey. This is stored in the beehive within a comb made of a waxy substance, and provides food in the winter for the honeybee larvae. Often the honeycomb is removed and the honey extracted by beekeepers. Delicious heather honey can be found on sale throughout Yorkshire.

S ean and Alison Franklin started brewing in 1982 and opened Franklins Brewery. After selling up they had a three year break before starting Roosters Brewery in 1993. They began by brewing eight barrels a week and that has now increased to forty, producing seven regular beers plus seasonal specials. Wanting to experiment with different brews they formed the Outlaw Brewing Company six months later operating from the same premises. This enables them to experiment using many varieties of hops and malt and creating individual beers some of which may become regulars under the Roosters label.

"Yea! Oh Yea!" - rang out the cry
That echoed round the square.
"I have a great announcement
Of such a perfect beer!"
Folk came running down the street
They'd heard the awful din,
Saw Town Crier wi' his bells
And quickly followed him.
They crowded in t' local pub
And filled the six bells full
And soon their heads were ringing
With good strong alcohol!

It is hard to imagine life nowadays without a telephone and we take for granted how easy it is to communicate our messages. Centuries ago the only way of getting your message across to a large number of people was to make as much noise as possible and yell at the top of your voice. The custom of ringing a bell to draw attention goes back centuries. The earliest evidence of the hand bell is a cast bronze bell that was found in Neneveh, (modern Iraq) and has been dated back to 655 B.C. In ancient Greece the hand bell was rung to announce the start of the markets and in ancient Rome to announce the opening of the baths.

Even in these modern times, a bell is still rung in Fernandes Brewery Tap to announce a birthday, where the lucky person is invited to down a half yard of ale! The challenge attracts those who must be as aged as Methusula as each week they claim to be yet another year older! Maybe the production of a birth certificate is called for! Several have managed to down the glass in one go, the quickest I have seen was in 16 seconds, but many a drop has been spilt as the bubble in the long glass rises to the rim, soaking the drinker with delicious beer!

At the old mill by the steam
Young Nellie had a swim,
The farmers boy was passing by,
She had not noticed him.
He'd been drinking at the pub
And had his fill of booze,
Then fallen by the riverside
To have a little snooze.
But when he woke and saw her
In all her nakedness,
He wished that he had left the pub
And drank a little less!

ABV
3.5%

"There's an old mill by the stream...Nellie Dean." So the old song goes. It was written in 1905 by American songwriter Henry Armstrong and is still around nearly 100 years later. My mother-in-law remembers being taken to the Palace Theatre, Manchester Road, Bradford by her grandfather in 1920 and hearing Nellie Wallace singing the song. It was usually performed at the end of the show alerting the audience that the pubs would soon be closing and last orders were being called. Nowadays, you can still hear it being sung, if not at an old time music hall, in pubs at closing time after a rowdy night.

OLD MILL BREWERY

Nellie Dene

ABV 3.5%

Bitter

The Old Mill Brewery is housed in an 18th century former malt kiln and corn mill in the market town of Snaith, North Yorkshire. The local Historical Society reveals the existence of breweries and maltsters within the town up to the last century. It wasn't until 1983 that brewing recommenced in Snaith with the establishment of the Old Mill Brewery. In 1991 a new brew house, equipped with a highly specified modern brewing plant, was installed. The Old Mill Brewery is dedicated to producing a range of quality real ales, not only for the local market but also through an extensive free trade network. Nellie Dean has recently been upgraded to 4.2%.

Pub t'was heavin', folk were slumped,
Their bellies full of ale,
The landlord pulled another pint,
The till rang up the sale.
His weary eyes glanced at the clock
T'was nearly closing time,
He'd only had a cuppa tea
And that was half past nine.
He called out "Sup yer pints up lads!
At home y'will be missed."
Then he slammed the pub door shut,
And merrily got pissed.

Early English common law imposed responsibility for the well being of travellers of the country's road upon inns and taverns. Any establishment that provided food and drink was given a licence to sell their wares in agreement to receive all travellers into their houses. These houses became known as public houses where one could rest and be nourished in return for a payment. The licensee of the public house was referred to as 'the landlord' as it was he who was in a position of authority over his household and all that entered. Until the 20th century public houses were owned by the landlord, however, in today's society many landlords are tenants, or guests themselves.

In 1858 Timothy Taylor began brewing beer in Cook Lane in the West Riding town of Keighley. In 1863 he set up and built a larger brewery at Knowle Spring where the company has remained ever since. The superb spring water that wells up from deep under the Pennines is still used today to produce the very best traditional cask ales. Since 1928 Timothy Taylor's beers have won over 70 prestigious honours at the Brewing Industry International Awards and Great British Beer Festivals. Apart from a most successful brewing business, the company owns 24 pubs in the Keighley area. 'Landlord' can be found on the pumps at pubs all over the country.

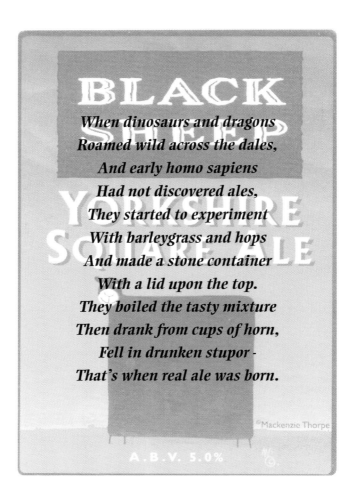

BLACK SHEEP

YORKSHIRE SQUARE ALE

When dinosaurs and dragons
Roamed wild across the dales,
And early homo sapiens
Had not discovered ales,
They started to experiment
With barleygrass and hops
And made a stone container
With a lid upon the top.
They boiled the tasty mixture
Then drank from cups of horn,
Fell in drunken stupor -
That's when real ale was born.

©Mackenzie Thorpe

A.B.V. 5.0%

B lack Sheep Brewery at Masham is in the centre of one of the most beautiful areas of Yorkshire. Surrounded by dales and moors it is within easy reach of many historical sites including ruins of Jervaulx Abbey and Fountains Abbey. To the north is Richmond with it's Norman castle and cobbled marketplace. To the west you enter Wensleydale, famous for it's cheese. Travelling east you enter James Herriot country, the setting for the series and film All Creatures Great and Small. Travelling south to Knaresborough you can see Mother Shipton's Cave where an array of objects hang solidified by lime in the water.

BLACK SHEEP

YORKSHIRE SQUARE ALE

©Mackenzie Thorpe

A.B.V. 5.0%

Before the introduction of stainless steel for the construction of fermentation vessels, stone slabs were used. These were referred to as Yorkshire squares as they were mostly extracted from Yorkshire quarries. Four large slabs of stone would be secured to form a square with a fifth for the base. A second larger square would surround the first leaving a gap between them for either cool or warm liquid to pass between them, thus controlling the temperature inside the block. By the 20th century slate replaced the stone and eventually aluminium was used for easier cleaning. Black Sheep Brewery is one of the few breweries who still use the traditional slate squares.

One cold dark night in winter
The stars shone up above,
They lit the way for Percy
On his way to the pub.
He went into the tavern
And stayed an hour or two,
Warmed the cockles of his heart
With mighty Old Bear brew.
He walked out in the moonlight
And staggered down the lane.
Bumped into a lamp post
Then saw the stars again!

Ursa Minor, latin for Little Bear, is a constellation of seven stars in the northern sky, including the Pole Star (Polaris), the brightest. This star has been the guiding light for travellers of land and sea for centuries and marks the position of the northern celestial pole. It is close to the constellation Ursa Major,(Great Bear), also known as the Plough or Great Dipper. Two of it's stars, the Pointers, are in a direct line with the Pole Star. Handy to know if you get lost after a heavy session at the pub and you need to find your way home!

Ursa Minor
ABV 4.5%
Old Bear Brewery

The Old Bear Brewery was set up by Brian Eastell in 1993 and in 1999 Keith Allatt took over the brewing. The brewery is in what was the stables of The Old White Bear pub at Cross Hills near Keighley. The pub was originally a coaching house in 1735 and has a wealth of huge oak beams which originally came from an old ship called the 'Old White Bear'. (A hint of this historical note can be seen on the pub sign where a picture of a ship is shown). Beams from the same ship were also used in the building of the Old White Bear at Halifax.

Jed was supping up his pint
He'd had a jar or two,
When the stranger staggered by
On his horse, Old Blue.
The Stranger fell down to the ground,
His face was ahen white,
He whispered, "Partner, help me quick
I need some ale tonight."
Jed rushed over to the bar
And bought the man a drink,
He said "Now sup up laddie,
You'll soon feel in the pink!"

I have found by writing this book that many beers are named on the spur of the moment, and not for any specific reason. For instance, Pale Rider, a well known Yorkshire beer, was named by one of the brewers after watching the film of the same name starring Clint Eastwood! David Wickett, the brewery owner tells me he believes that Clint brews a beer of the same name in California that has been registered in the U.S.A, although I imagine the brewing is done for him. Should Mr Eastwood need any advice on brewing I am sure David Wickett will be only too pleased to take a trip to California to compare notes!

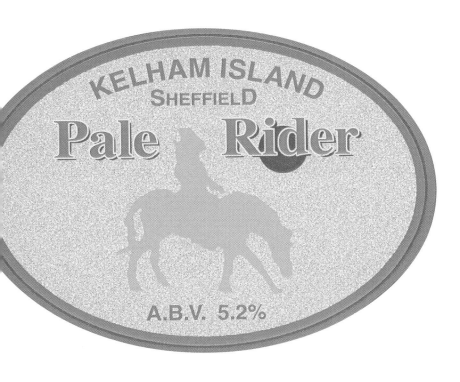

Kelham Island brewery was started by David Wicket in 1990. It was originally intended to be a small specialised operation as there were already four large breweries in Sheffield. However, after the closure of the big four, Kelham Island survived and is now the biggest. The original brewery was at the side of the Fat Cat pub in Alma Street, but has now expanded and moved over the road. The Fat Cat, a separate company, continues to attract lovers of real ale, serving a wide variety of Kelham Island beers. Visitors to the brewery can arrange to tour the visitors centre where a range of beer memorabilia is housed.

There stands an ancient building
Along a Yorkshire street
A place that smells of malt and hops
Where local folk would meet.
Since the eighteenth century
It's brought the country cheer,
In the great tradition
Of brewing Yorkshire beer.
When you're feeling thirsty
Wherever you may be,
You're sure to find a pint of ale
From Sam Smith's brewery.

The Old Brewery at Tadcaster was established in 1758 and brews at the oldest brewery in Yorkshire. Samuel Smith's is a small independent brewery and uses traditional methods of brewing. The water is still drawn from the original well sunk 85 feet underground, then mixed with the malt in copper mash-tuns. The yeast is a strain that has been used since the beginning of the last century producing a rich creamy head to the beer. The ale is fermented in roofed fermenting vessels made of solid blocks of slate. The brewery even has its own cooper who makes and repairs all the wooden casks used for the brewery's naturally conditioned Old Brewery Bitter, 4% a.b.v.

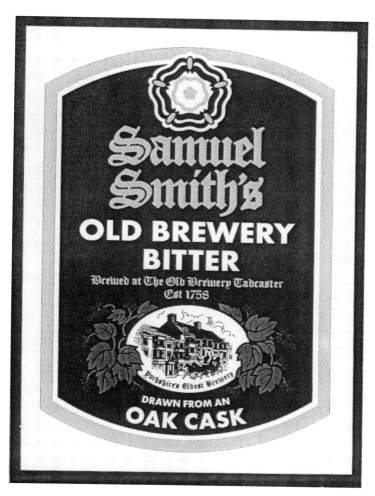

Samuel Smith's is the smallest of the three breweries in Tadcaster. One of the attractions at the brewery are the grey Shire horses kept at the stables. Before the days of the motor engine, horses were used widely in almost every industry including the brewing trade. Nowadays Samuel Smith's Shires make occasional deliveries of beer to a couple of pubs in the town, the sound of their hooves on the Tadcaster streets echoing the past. A visit to the stables to see these magnificent creatures is not to be missed. The sheer size of them, about eight feet tall, is overwhelming. To see them in action pulling the dray through the busy streets is to take a step back in time.

The Boat Brewery

Sam had had too much to drink,
He'd got a thumping head.
The captain of the riverboat
Told him to swing the lead.
"We need to find a 4.5!"
The captain roared at Sam,
"Now chuck that rope overboard
As fast now as you can!"
Sam hid from view, half asleep,
He swung the rope around
But didn't check the water's depth
And so they went aground.

BY THE MARK 4.5%

Choosing a pump clip from Ron's extensive collection was quite a task. Many of his brews are one offs, By the Mark 4.5% being one of them. You'll notice the weight on the end of the rope and may have heard the term 'swinging the lead'. When the boatmen wanted to check the depth of the river they would throw out a weighted rope marked in feet. When the weight hit the bottom they could tell how deep the water was. This was a tiresome task and many would just swing the rope not dropping it in the water. Hence 'swinging the lead' became a term for someone who makes excuses to escape work.

When brewer Ron Ridout retired from the chemical industry he decided to open his own brewery turning a hobby into a business. His association with Brian Lockwood, owner of the Boat pub at Allerton-by-Water near Castleford, offered the opportunity to brew in the old stables at the rear of the pub. The Boat is 300 years old and is the oldest building in the village. A painting in the bar shows the original boat that used to bring the miners across the river Aire to Allerton-by-Water coalmine and take men back to Saville pit in Methley for just a half penny, in those days, the price of a pint.

Wild storms across the ocean,
Had washed a raft ashore.
The local men were fearful,
Their country was at war.
They seized the sole survivor
Who spoke in foreign tongue,
And in their drunken frenzy
Said "All spies should be hung!"
The stranger was defenceless
They hoisted him up high,
"Who has hung that monkey?"
"We thought he was a spy!"

In the old English seaport of Hartlepool, the local people tell of a strange legend. Many centuries ago when Britain was at war, a monkey was found clinging to a raft that had been washed ashore. The poor creature, chattering from cold and fright, was believed to been speaking a foreign language. Thought to be a spy, the monkey was arrested and met an untimely end. If you are ever in Hartlepool, never say to a local 'Who hung the monkey'. It may be taken as an insult to their judgment! This beer was brewed in support of monkeys.

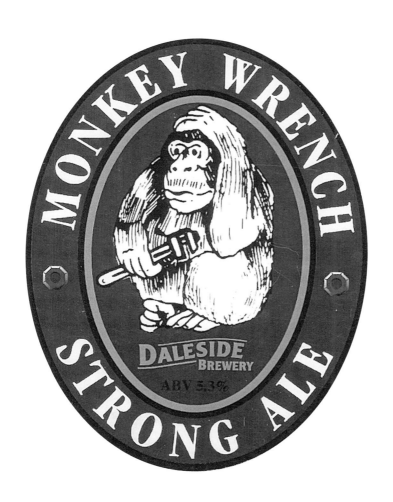

D aleside Brewery produces a wide range of excellent cask conditioned ales. All cask ales are live, unblended and 'real'. This quality is extended to it's bottled beers where care is taken to maintain flavour, colour and strength whilst giving a reasonable shelf life. Only best quality ingredients are used, top quality malts and full leaf hops, and of course the spa water from nearby Harrogate which is well known for it's medicinal qualities. No pellets, sugars, drops, hop oils or malt extracts are used in the brewing process.

Bill was coming from the pub
He'd had a lovely night,
When walking home along the road
He had a shocking fright.
For there before him stood a thing
It towered ten feet high,
With hairy legs and armpits
And scarlet piercing eyes.
"Oh heck!" he cried in terror,
"That beers gone to my head!
Please go away I promise I'll
Drink lemonade instead!"

The Gryphon, or Griffin, is a mythological creature with the head of an eagle and the body of a lion, sometimes depicted with wings. Paired with the Egyptian sphinx, it is thought to have been a sacred image although its exact place in cult and legend is unknown. Statues have been found dating as far back as the late bronze age and at Knossos in Crete the gryphon is pictured in paintings surrounding ritual chambers. Combining the strength of a lion with the keen eye of the eagle it was used as a symbol of protection. In heraldry the gryphon depicts honour and achievement. 'Rampant' depicts the gryphon on hind legs, side view, 'Guardant', full faced.

W entworth Brewery was built using equipment from the old Stones and Wards breweries and launched it's first beer in September 1999. To date it has won nine different CAMRA awards. It operates in the old powerhouse in Wentworth which 100 years ago housed steam generators creating electricity for Wentworth Woodhouse. This stately home has the largest frontage of any stately home in Europe. The name for the brewery was inspired by the gryphon shown on the Wentworth coat of arms. The brewery is currently looking for a location for its own brewery tap.

T'was Halloween, the moon was full
And shone bright all around,
The shadow of old Elsie witch
Fell sharply on the ground.
She swooped across the heavens,
Then saw a place she knew
To park her battered broomstick
And stop off for a brew.
She went inside the tavern
Then swilled back several pints,
"Ahaa!" she cackled loudly,
"There'll be no spells tonight!"

Halloween originates from a custom of the ancient Celts who worshipped gods of nature. The 31st October marked the end of the season of the sun and the coming of the season of darkness. They believed that in winter the sun god was taken prisoner by Samhain, the Lord of the Dead, who would call up the deceased to take on new forms, the most evil being a cat. They would hold festivals in the woods and witches would arrive on their broomsticks, along with their cats, causing mischief and casting spells. It was believed that if you put your clothes on inside out and walk backwards on Halloween you would meet a witch. Take care not to get that drunk on Halloween!

After an absence of four years from the brewing scene Goose Eye was re-opened in 1991 in a converted warehouse. Slowly expanding, it now supplies around 75 free trade outlets in North and West Yorkshire, Lancashire, Manchester and Merseyside. The beers are also available through national wholesalers. Goose Eye's seasonal and occasional beers are proving very successful. Goose Eye is owned by father and son Jack and David Atkinson who are committed to brewing traditional additive free beers with the emphasis on consistency. There are 5 regular beers available and always a special brew.

The grist was mashed, hops were boiled,
The brewer settled down,
With glass in hand he waited for
His lass to come from town.
The brew it boiled to perfect pitch,
He left it to ferment,
Then tried a sample from the cask
But drank more than he meant.
His lass arrived a little late
To find him on the floor,
"You'll be no use to me, you've had
Too much of Marston Moor!"

T he term 'brewer's droop' is well known for describing lack of specific body response after drinking too much alcohol and the naming of Brewers Droop beer is not quite as romantic's the poem written for it. Peter Smith, the owner and brewer, let me into the secret of the real reason. During the brewing of a new beer, the plates in the mash tank collapsed and the whole contents disappeared down a big hole! Hence the recipe was named Brewers Droop! But with a 5% strength and a moreish taste, I would tend to note the effects described in the poem should you drink too much before that special occasion.

Marston Moor first started brewing in 1983 and took it's name from the great battlefield of Marston Moor where the first brewery was situated. In 1988 it moved to it's current location at the rear of the old Crown public house in the small village of Kirk Hammerton near York. The pub closed in 1993 but brewing continued. In addition to brewing a range of beers from 3.6% to 5%. Peter Smith, the owner, also acts as a consultant to micro-brewers in Britian and abroad. Apart from teaching the art of brewing real ale, Peter has built breweries in other countries including Hungary and Jersey.

Prospectors came from far and wide,
They'd heard of Yorkshire Gold.
Bearing spades and shovels
They dug where they were told.
For weeks they shovelled madly,
The sweat poured from their heads,
Then old Horace said out loud
"Lets have some beer instead!"
They went off to the local pub
And drank till they were cool.
"At last we've found our pots of gold
We've all been great big fools!"

Fools Gold, also known as pyrite, is a natural iron mineral. The gold flecks in the rock appear to give the appearance of a gold nugget and many a prospector thought he had found his fortune. The name pyrite comes from the Greek pyr, meaning fire, because it sparks when struck against steel. It is for this property that it is used in wheel lock guns where a serrated wheel rotates against it causing a spark that ignites the explosive. It is also used commercially as a source of sulphur to produce sulphuric acid. Pyrite has been found in pre-historic burial grounds.

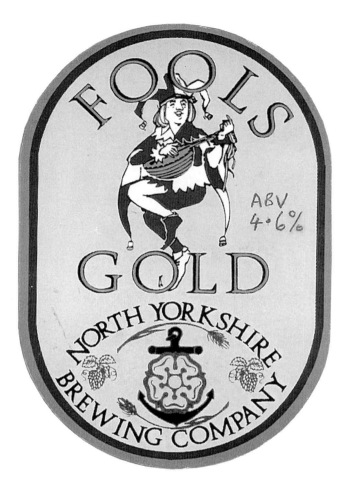

FOOLS GOLD

ABV 4·6%

NORTH YORKSHIRE BREWING COMPANY

George Tinsley started the North Yorkshire Brewing Company in 1989 in a warehouse behind a small terrace shop in Middlesborough. Looking for larger premises he sold his two pubs and moved to Pinchinthorpe Hall, a listed medieval ancient monument near Guisborough. This was the ideal location to expand the brewery and new copper vessels were installed. Having it's own natural spring, the brewery follows traditional methods and has just acquired certification of organic brewing. Pinchinthorpe Hall also has a hotel and restaurant.

Jack donned his cap, kissed the wife,
"I'm off t'pub," he said,
"If I'm not back by nightfall
Just you go off t'bed."
He went down to his local
And drank till half past one,
He'd had a few too many when
The moon blocked out the sun.
"Hey up! What going on here?
I've not been here all night!
I'd best be getting home now
Or I'm in for a fight!"

The pub was renamed the Rat & Ratchet by a group of CAMRA members and has nothing to do with rats in the cellar! Because of the name of the pub, Andrew has based the names of his brews on the rat theme. Obscuratis 3.7% abv, was brewed to commemorate the total eclipse of the sun in July 1999. It was a warm sunny day, perfect for viewing the eclipse over Britain. As the moon slowly moved between the earth and the sun, day turned to night and the air turned icy cold. During a total eclipse the Earths atmosphere produces a weird effect and it is said that men and animals react with fear to this phenomenon. Not a good time to be drinking too much ale!

The Rat & Ratchet Brewery is a brew pub down Chapel Hill in
Huddersfield. It was started by Andrew Moorhouse who brews down
in the cellar. He has brewed around 50 beers since 1995. The original
pub dates back to 1866 and was called the Grey Horse Inn. Being next to
Grey Horse Yard it was probably an old coaching inn at the entrance of the
town. Chapel Hill was the subject of a Lowry painting and although Lowry
was focusing on the viaduct at the bottom of the hill, I am sure the Rat &
Ratchet features somewhere along the right hand side! The Lowry painting
can be seen in the Huddersfield Art Gallery.

The Romans were revolting
Up north in Danum town,
London had nicked all their ale
And drank the whole lot down.
They marched down to the city
And at the forum gates
Roared, "Give us back our barrels
Before it is too late!"
The Lords came from their houses
With tankards full of beer,
"To Yorkshire we surrender!"
The Romans cried, "Hear, hear!"

Around 54 B.C. Julius Caesar invaded Britain and the Roman Empire spread all over the country including South Yorkshire. One of the settlements became known as Danum, now called Doncaster. Danum Gold expresses the motto of the brewery, 'A speck of gold in a desert of mediocrity', being a golden colour and having an unique taste and aroma. In July 2001 local MP Mr Kevin Hughes, arranged for Danum Gold to be served at the Strangers Bar in the House of Commons, hence bringing a taste of a great Yorkshire ale to the city of London. At the time of writing, Glentworth Brewery is to be featured on North of Westminster. I am sure that the Romans would have approved!

GLENTWORTH BREWERY
Doncaster
Danum Gold
Cask Conditioned Real Ale
4.1%abv

Glentworth Brewery at Skellow near Doncaster was set up in 1996 by Geoff Brown. The brewery is located in the outbuildings originally designed and built as a dairy. All the infrastructure was already in place to convert to a brewing plant. Having large access doors, a high roof structure, drains, electricity and a cold room it was an ideal building for brewing beer. Although the brewery is owned by Geoff, the day to day management is done by brother-in-law Alan Hutchison. Glentworth Brewery provides a range of beers to 80 outlets covering Yorkshire, Lincolnshire, Derby and Nottingham.

"Hey! Stop thief!" the policeman cried
And jumped onto his bike,
Followed Greengrass down the lane
Till he was out of sight.
Four miles later, out of breath
A thought came to his head,
"I bet that rogue is in the pub!"
And to the inn he sped.
There he found him, pint in hand
And on his face a grin,
A pheasant in each pocket,
So he arrested him!

One of the most popular local programmes on Yorkshire TV is Heartbeat, set in the North Yorkshire Moors. The notorious character Greengrass, played by actor Bill Maynard, is a lovable rogue who can be found either poaching in the countryside or drinking at the Aidensfield Arms. This beer was actually named by the Old Rogue himself. A golden coloured beer, complex in taste with First Gold the main hop, it is described as having a teasing taste, rather like it's namesake.

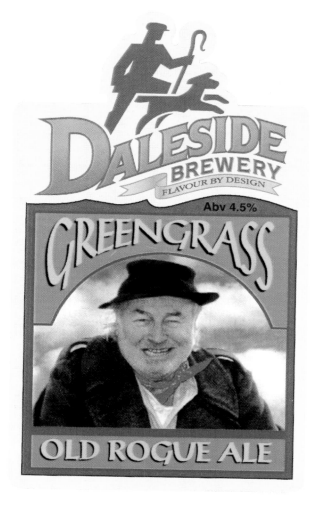

aleside not only produces fine cask ales but also produces several of it's range of beers in bottles. Bottled beers that do not appear in cask include Duff Beer 5.0 % abv, a dark strong beer with a dry finish and Ripon Jewel Ale 8%. abv, an amber beer with a fruity aroma. All the bottles have specially designed labels telling the story behind the beer. Special bottled beers have been produced exclusively for Booth's Supermarkets in the North West which was voted Beer Supermarket of the Year 2000.

T'was Molly's first time on't canal
She was not very keen
To leave her land legs on the bank
And be a trained marine.
But Herbert had insisted
They hired a narrow boat
And said that she would love it
When they both got afloat.
But Molly was so nervous,
That she took to drink,
Just to blot the memory
In case the boat should sink.

Originally built in 1700 the Aire and Calder Navigation linked the port of Goole with Leeds and was used mainly for transporting coal and raw wool. Nowadays, canal paths are an excellent way to explore the countryside. From Wakefield you can walk to Thornhill locks and at the Calder and Hebble junction take the Dewsbury Arm to Saville Town Basin where you will find the Leggers pub. Many of the tunnels were very low and narrow, the only way of passing under them was to get the barge through by human effort. Men would lay on their backs and propel the boat by pushing their feet under the roof of the tunnel, hence they were given the name 'leggers'.

CANAL
NO 7

ABV: 4.2%

Sunset Cider & Wine

The Sunset Cider & Wine Company originally started operating at Blackmoor Brewery near Batley and moved to it's present location, the Leggers pub in 1988. The Leggers was originally the old stable block at the Saville Town canal basin, (the brewery has a beer named after Marriot, a canal tow-horse that was stabled here). The hayloft was made into a pub where a relaxing homely atmosphere has been created with comfy sofas and an open fire. The boatyard is the only working boatyard in the area and many of the workshops are based alongside the brewery. There is also a small waterways museum.

Goose Eye Brewery

The frost was on the meadow,
The Christmas lights were lit,
Old Gertie Goose was peckin'
At worms and tasty bits.
But at the pub the farmer
Was bargaining a price,
Roast Gertie Goose for dinner
Would taste so very nice!
But when he came to catch her
To cook on Christmas day,
She hissed at him, spread her wings,
And promptly flew away!

Christmas Goose

Goose has always been a traditional meal for the festive season. This recipe was given to me by my 101 year old grandmother. Wash the goose inside and out. Season inside and out with salt and pepper. Put a piece of butter inside to keep it moist. It should not be stuffed with sage and onions. Brush with melted butter and roast 20 minutes at 350° for every pound with an extra 20 minutes at 400°. Serve with gravy and braised chestnuts. To braise chestnuts, make a slit in the side and put them in a tin in the oven for about 10 minutes. Remove the brown shells and the under skins. Put in a casserole, add a little salt and a teaspoon of sugar and a little goose fat to cover. Cook until the stock is reduced and glazes the chestnuts.

Goose Eye Brewery is situated in Keighley, West Yorkshire. Tours around the brewery are available by arrangement, and if you are a keen railway enthusiast, you might also like to take a trip on the Keighley and Worth Valley railway. The five mile line uses steam locomotives and several historic carriages, many of which have a real ale bar on board. Trains run between Oxenhope and Keighley, passing through the beautiful scenery of Bronte county at Haworth and Oakworth. The line is well known for it's part in the film The Railway Children. The Museum of Rail Travel is situated at Ingrow.

A learned scholar came to town
To search for wealth and fame.
He was a man of many words,
Will Shakespeare was his name.
"Wherefore art thou going sir?"
A voice behind him cried.
"Good Maid I yearn for liquid gold"
The maid said, "Come inside"
She led him to Fernandes,
The Landlord poured him ale,
It gave him inspiration,
Now, thereby lies a tale...

Many beers brewed at Fernandes Brewery Tap are named after pubs that used to be in Wakefield. Shakespeare Special Bitter is named after the Shakespeare Tavern that was located in Teal Street from 1887. William Shakespeare was born on the 26th April 1564 at Stratford-on-Avon and died 23rd April 1616. Shakespeare's father was an Ale Conner, equivalent to today's Custom and Excise Officer. The Ale Conner wore leather breeches and to check the strength of the beer would pour some ale on a bench and sit on it. How well the leather stuck to the wet bench would determine how much sugar was in the beer, and therefore reveal the content of alcohol. What a waste!

FERNANDES

SHAKESPEARE SB 3.4%

L ouis Fernandes was a Portuguese immigrant who came to England to make his fortune. He constructed and founded the original brewery in the early 1800's. It was acquired by John Smiths of Tadcaster in 1919 and the actual building sold to the Beverley Brewery. Later it was used as a malt store then a bottle store before Dave and Maureen James bought it in 1994. Maureen opened a brew shop on the ground floor, which is an Aladdin's cave for home brewers, and Dave started brewing in the cellar in 1996. In 1999 the upper floor was converted to a homely bar, where you can see Dave's wonderful collection of pub signs and beer trays.

A hard day at the office
Or factory or shop?
A weary time at work today
Where pressure never stops?
The boss has been demanding
Your head feels it may burst,
Your mouth is like a birdcage
You've got a raging thirst?
Well here's a small suggestion
To make you come alive,
Head off for a drink tonight
It's opening time at five!

The term 'Gimme five' originates in America and is commonly used as a greeting in the slapping of hands. When investigating other instances of the number 5 you will find it is represented in many other areas, for instance: there are 5 main horse races - the Derby, Oaks, St Leger, 1,000 guineas and 2,000 guineas. There are 5 self-born Buddhas that have existed since the beginning of time, each representing the 5 skandas that make up the entire cosmos. In Greek mythology, 5 sisters who nursed the wine god Dionysus were rewarded by being made into the five stars of the constellation Pleiades. And so it goes on. Pick a number and try it for yourself!

For over 1200 years hops have been used for brewing ale. The common hop grows to about 26 feet long and when ripe, the flowers are picked and dried ready for brewing. The bitterness of the beer produced depends on soft resins and essential oils contained in the hops. They are boiled with malt to release the bitterness, then a different type of hop is added later in the process to give an aroma to the brew. Varying tastes can be acquired by using different types from different areas. Gimme Five has been brewed using five different types, Green Bullet, Chinook, Styring Goldings, Hallertau New Zealand and Wilhamet.

Alf was such a grumpy man
His heart was black as coal,
His poor wife suffered constantly
From his troubled soul.
"Now come on Alf," she said to him,
And took him by the arm,
"Sit down and have a pint of ale,
Relax and takes things calm"
Soon Alf was feeling better,
A smile came to his face
She thought, "He's not so bad now,
His hearts in the right place."

Black Heart, is a black stout with a roasted malt flavour was named by the company manager to reflect it's dark rich colour. A tropical climbing plant called the Balloon Vine is sometimes referred to as Black Heart due to the big bladder-like seed pods that contain black seeds with a white heart shaped spot. Black Heart is also a card game developed in the USA over a century ago. It is played with two sets of cards with all diamonds, jacks, queens and kings of hearts removed and black jokers added to make a deck of 75 cards. Sir Henry Rider-Haggard, better known for writing King Solomon's Mines, also wrote a book called Black Heart-White Heart, which tells the love story of a white English missionary and a black African woman.

The Barnsley Brewing Co. Ltd. operates from a purpose built brewery within the Elsecar Heritage Centre, Wath Road, Elsecar near Barnsley. The Heritage Centre is well worth a visit and includes The Powerhouse, an interactive display of power and energy. For those interested in beer memorabilia there is a small museum called Codswallop which has a magnificent display of bottles, labels, casks and hundreds of other interesting general breweriana. A steam railway runs from the Centre through a conservation area to Hemmingfield Halt along the Elsecar branch of the Deane and Dove canal.

DENT BREWERY

Shirley Sheep was scared to death
Her fleece it stood on end,
Chris Tarrant said, "Now Shirley love,
D'you want to phone a friend?
This question is worth lots of brass,
Just take your time and think.
What does every Yorkshire man
Like for his favourite drink?"
Shirley paused, and scratched her head,
She ba'ad, "A pint of beer."
"Well done!" said Chris, "I think ewe are
The first sheep millionaire!"

4.5% ABV

EWE WANTS TO BE A MILLIONAIRE

The programme 'Who wants to be a millionaire', hosted by Chris Tarrant, was first broadcasted by ITV on 4th September 1998. Since then it has become one of the most popular quiz shows on television, the format being exported all over the world to 80 countries. On November 20th 2000, Judith Keppel became the show's first millionaire, and more recently David Edwards became the second on 21st April 2001. Incidently, had Jim Titmuss, who was going for £250,000, read this book before the show, he would have known that Dick Turpin was hung at York and would not have lost £93,000!

Although technically in Cumbria, I have included Dent Brewery in this Yorkshire Pumpclip collection because many local residents feel they still belong to Yorkshire. Until 1974 Yorkshire was divided into three separate Ridings – North, East, and West Riding. People living in the former East Riding have successfully campaigned to create East Yorkshire, but locals around Dent remain firmly in Cumbria. Dent Brewery was started by Martin Stafford, originally to supply beer to the two brewery pubs in the village. The beer was so popular that it was soon operating at capacity in order to provide beer for pubs throughout the Yorkshire Dales and Lake District.

Poor Joe was lying on his bed,
His brow was full of sweat.
He groaned "I think my time is up
But I can't go just yet."
His wife said "I'll get vicar love
T'come and give last rites"
Joe said "No, go get me coat,
I'll go for my last pint."
He staggered to the tavern
And downed a pint or two,
Said, "Go and cancel vicar love,
I'm feeling rite brand new!"

Since time began, performing the 'last rites' upon the dying has been part of the existence of living things. The procedure can even been seen in the animal kingdom as the pack will gather around a dying creature and perform a ritual not unlike that of humans. In many religions it is regarded as an important occasion where the soul of the dying must be prepared for death. In ancient China the body was washed, nails trimmed and head shaved. Similarly in Egypt the preparation was meticulously carried out. In many religions the ritual of last rites is regarded as a preparation for leaving this world and entering the next, cleansed and pure and...SOBER??

Abbeydale Brewery was started by Patrick Morton in 1996. Situated in Sheffield it gets it's name from Beauchief Abbey nearby which now lies in ruins. As with many Independent breweries producing excellent real ales, Abbeydale operates from a small unit and brews a good range of beers. It supplies around 100 pubs with guest beers and maintains it's emphasis on quality and interesting flavours using the soft water of the Sheffield area which is perfect for the brewing process. Other ales along the Abbey theme include Moonshine 4.3% Archangel 4.7% and Black Mass 6.66%.

The Calder and Hebble Junction.

Autumn colours adorn the hills and dales of Yorkshire.

Could this be the ghost of the Black Dog as he sits waiting patiently for his master, Dracula to return from the Graveyard at Whitby Abbey?

Grosmont Station is the terminus for the North Yorkshire railway and has been restored to the British Railways style of the 1960's.

The Kilburn white horse in the Hambleton Hills can be seen from miles away.

Dewsbury Minster bell tower still rings out as Black Tom tolls each Christmas Eve.

'Double Chance' winner of the 1925 Grand National. (Photograph by kind permission of Malton Brewery)

The Mexborough Concertina Band photographed in 1923. (Photograph by kind permission of The Concertina Brewery)

	Telephone No.	Fax No.
ABBEYDALE BREWERY Unit 8, Aizlewood Rd. Sheffield, S Yorks. S8 0YX	0114 2812712	0114 2812713
ANGLO DUTCH BREWERY Unit 12, Saville Bridge Mills, Mill St. East, Dewsbury, W. Yorks WF12 6QQ	01924 457772	
BARGE & BARREL BREWERY Co. 10-20 Park Road, Elland, W Yorks. HX5 9HP	01422 375039	
BARNSLEY BREWING COMPANY LTD Elsecar, Barnsley, S. Yorks	01226 741010	01226 741009
BLACK DOG BREWERY St Hilda Business Centre, The Ropery, Whitby, N Yorks. YO22 4EU	01947 821467	01947 603301
BLACK SHEEP BREWERY PLC Wellgarth, Masham, Ripon, N Yorks. HG4 4EN	01765 689227	01765 689746
BOAT BREWERY The Boat Inn, Off Main Street Allerton by Water, W Yorks. WF10 2BX	01977 667788	
BRISCOE'S BREWERY 16 Ash Grove, Otley, W Yorks. LS21 3EL	01943 466515	01943 466515
BROWN COW BREWERY Brown Cow Road, Barlow, Selby, N Yorks. YO8 8EH	01757 618947	01757 618947
HB CLARK Co (Successors) Ltd. Westgate Brewery, Wakefield, W Yorks. WF2 9SW	01924 373328	01924 372306

	Telephone No.	Fax No.
CONCERTINA BREWERY 9A Dolcliffe Rd, Mexborough, S Yorks. S64 9AZ	01709 580841	
CROPTON BREWERY Woolcroft, Cropton, Nr.Pickering, N.Yorks YO18 8HH	01751 417330	01751 417310
DALESIDE BREWERY Unit 1Carnwal Road, Starbeck, Harrogate N Yorks. HG1 4PT	01423 880022	01423 541717
DENT BREWERY Hollins, Cowgill Dent, Cumbria LA10 5TQ	01539 625326	01539 625033
FERNANDES BREWERY The Old Malt House, 5 Avisons Yard, Kirkgate Wakefield. W Yorks WF1 1UA	01924 291709	
GLENTWORTH BREWERY Glentworth House, Crossfield Lane, Skellow, Doncaster, S Yorks. DN6 8PL	01302 725555	01302 724133
GOOSE EYE BREWERY Ingrow Bridge, South St. Keighley, W Yorks. BD22 5AX	01535 605807	01535 605735
HAMBLETON ALES Holme-on-Swale, Thirsk, N Yorks. YO7 4JE	01845 567460	01845 567741
THE HULL BREWERY Co Ltd. 144-148 English St. Hull, E Yorks. HU3 2BT	01482 586364	01482 586 365

	Telephone No.	Fax No.
KELHAM ISLAND BREWERY Ltd 23 Alma St. Sheffield, S Yorks. S3 8SA	01142 494808	0114 2494803
LINFIT BREWERY 139 Lane Top, Linthwaite, Huddersfield, W Yorks. HD7 5SG	01484 842370	
MALTON BREWERY Co. Ltd. 12 Wheelgate, Malton, N Yorks. YO17 7HP	01653 697580	01653 691812
MARSTON MOOR BREWERY Crown House, Kirk Hammerton, York , N Yorks.YO26 8DD	01423 330341	01423 330341
NORTH YORKSHIRE BREWING Co. Pinchinthorpe Hall, Pinchinthorpe, Guisborough, N Yorks NY4 8HG	01287 630200	
OLD BEAR BREWERY 6 Keighley Road, Cross Hills Keighley, W Yorks BD20 7RN	01535 632115	
OLD MILL BREWERY Ltd Mill St. Snaith, Goole, E Yorks. DN14 9HU	01405 861813	01405 862789
OSSETT BREWERY Brewers Pride, Healey Rd Ossett, West Yorkshire. WF5	01924 261333	
RAT & RATCHET Chapel Hill, Huddersfield W Yorks. HD1 3ED	01484 516734	
RIVERHEAD 2 Peel St. Marsden, Huddersfield, W Yorks. HD7 6BR	01484 841270	

	Telephone No.	Fax No.

ROOSTERS
Unit 20 Claro Court Business Centre.
Claro Rd, Harrogate
N Yorks. HG1 4BA

01423 561861   01423 561861

RUDGATE
2 Centre Park, Marston Business Centre
Rudgate, Tockwith.
York, N Yorks. YO26 7QF

01423 358382   01423 358382

SALAMANDER
22 Harry Street, Bradford
W Yorks. BD4 9PH

01274 652323

SAMUEL SMITH
The Old Brewery, High Street
Tadcaster, N Yorks. LS24 9SB

01937 832225   01937 834673

SUNSET CIDER & WINE Ltd.,
The Leggers Inn, Saville Wharf
Mill Street East, Dewsbury
W Yorks. WF12 9BD

01924 502846

TIMOTHY TAYLOR & Co Ltd.,
Knowles Spring Brewery,
Belina Street, Keighley
W Yorks. BD21 1AW

01535 603139   01535 691167

TURKEY BREWERY
The Turkey Inn,
Goose Eye, Keighley
W Yorks.

01535 681339

WENTWORTH BREWERY Ltd.,
The Powerhouse,
The Gun Park, Wentworth
S Yorks. S62 7TF

01226 747070   10226 747050

YORK BREWERY Co Ltd.,
12 Toft Green, Micklegate,
York, N Yorks. YO1 6JT

01904 621162   01904 6221126

ACKNOWLEDGEMENTS

The author would like to thank all the breweries featured in this book. Without their help and time it could never have been written. I would particularly like to mention Eric Lucas at Daleside who was my first contact and gave me the confidence to approach other breweries, David James and all my drinking pals at Fernandes Brewery Tap who encouraged me through all the doubtful moments when I thought it would never be published.

A special thanks to my husband Chris. Without his influence I would never have found real ale. (If you can't beat them, join them!) He is my best friend and my biggest critic. Writing this book has cost him several pints in carrying out the research and I'm proud of him for sitting in the car, resisting sampling the beers from the breweries because he was 'driving Miss Rosie!'

111